Bankers' secrets

How the banks control our financial lives ?

Contents

Regulation and Banking Supervision 35

Typology of banking risks 42

Risk Management Techniques 50

The Bank and Monetary Policy 56

Banks and Financial Markets 62

History and Evolution of Banks

The First Banks

The first banks date back several millennia before our era, in the civilizations of Mesopotamia, Egypt, and ancient Greece. However, these banks were very different from the ones we know today.

Ancient banks had functions similar to modern banks, including deposit management, loans, and foreign exchange operations. However, their activity was based on the exchange of goods and precious metals rather than currency. Furthermore, banks were often owned by wealthy merchants or religious temples.

In the Middle Ages, Italian bankers established the first modern banks. Italian merchants began using letters of credit to facilitate trade between different regions of Europe. These letters of credit allowed merchants to transfer funds from one account to another without having to transport coins.

In the following centuries, banks evolved into more formal and regulated institutions. Central banks were created to help stabilize national economies, while commercial banks began offering a wider range of financial services, such as mortgages and credit cards.

Major banking crises have also had a significant impact on the history of banks. The 1929 financial crisis in the United States led to the bankruptcy of many banks and led to the creation of the Federal Deposit Insurance Corporation (FDIC), a deposit insurance system that guarantees bank deposits up to a certain limit. In 2008, the global financial crisis highlighted the significant risks associated with banking activities, such as risky loans and complex derivative products.

The Birth of Modern Banks

The birth of modern banks is a key moment in economic and financial history. It occurred at the end of the Middle Ages when the first international trade began to develop. During this time, merchants needed to finance their commercial operations, but they could not do so using their own capital. This is how the first banks came into existence.

These banks were often family businesses run by wealthy and influential merchants. They began offering financial services such as deposit management, money transfers, and commercial loans. Modern banks also started issuing banknotes, which were often exchangeable for gold or silver.

Modern banks experienced significant growth from the 18th century onwards with the rise of the Industrial Revolution and the market economy. Banks quickly diversified, offering services such as wealth management, mortgages, and insurance.

One of the most significant developments in the modern banking sector was the creation of central banks. These institutions were established to regulate the money supply in the economy and prevent financial crises. The first central banks were created in the 17th century in Europe, but they expanded considerably in the 20th century with the creation of the Federal Reserve in the United States and the European Central Bank.

The advent of computing and digital technologies also transformed the modern banking sector. Banks started offering online services and using technologies such as blockchain to improve the security and speed of transactions. Banks also had to adapt to new regulations related to cybersecurity and the protection of personal data.

Major Banking and Financial Crises

Major banking and financial crises have marked the history of the global economy and have deeply affected the financial systems of countries. They have also had repercussions on the daily lives of ordinary citizens. The most famous of these is the 1929 crisis, which led to the Great Depression and had a global impact.

The 1929 crisis was caused by a speculative bubble in stock markets and overproduction in industry. When the bubble burst, many investors lost all their money, and companies had to lay off workers on a massive scale. This led to a reduction in the demand for goods and services, resulting in a global economic recession.

More recently, the 2008 global financial crisis was caused by a housing bubble in the United States, where banks were granting mortgages to people who could not afford to repay them. These loans were bundled into complex financial products called «subprime mortgages» and sold on global financial markets. When the housing bubble burst and the loans began to default, banks incurred massive losses, leading to a crisis of confidence in the global financial system.

These crises highlighted the importance of effective regulation and supervision of the banking sector. Since the 2008 crisis, many reforms have been undertaken to strengthen bank regulation and oversight. Prudential regulations, such as the Basel Accords, have been strengthened to improve the solvency and liquidity of banks. Deposit guarantee and crisis resolution systems have also been put in place to protect customers and taxpayers.

It is important to note that financial crises are not inevitable, and financial stability can be maintained through appropriate regulation and supervision. Banks play a crucial role in the economy by financing businesses and households, creating money, and providing essential financial services. Therefore, maintaining a strong and stable banking system is crucial to ensure sustainable economic growth and prosperity for all.

Role and Functions of Banks in the Economy

Interconnection with the Global Economic System

Banks are key players in the global economic system. They interact with businesses, individuals, and governments to provide essential financial services such as economy finance, currency management, and protection against financial risks. Their role in the economic system is crucial as they are responsible for the creation and circulation of currency, which is at the foundation of all economic transactions.

Banks interact with the global economy in various ways. Firstly, they offer financial services to businesses and individuals that are active in local, regional, and global economies. Commercial banks provide loans and credit to assist businesses in getting started and expanding, while investment banks offer advisory and financing services to large corporations seeking global expansion.

Banks also interact with governments by purchasing government bonds and participating in financing programs to assist governments in funding infrastructure projects and supporting the economy. Central banks play a particularly important role in the interconnection with the global economic system as they are responsible for monetary policy and financial stability. They intervene in the markets to regulate inflation and economic growth and to maintain financial stability during times of crisis.

Furthermore, banks interact with global financial markets. Investment banks are significant players in financial markets, where they buy and sell stocks, bonds, and derivatives. Commercial banks utilize financial markets for financing and managing risks related to their activities. Central banks also interact with financial markets by buying and selling assets to regulate inflation and economic growth.

Lastly, banks interact with other actors in the global economic system, such as international financial institutions, regulatory bodies, and supervisory organizations. Development banks, for example, work with international financial institutions to provide long-term financing to developing countries. Regulatory and supervisory bodies work with banks to ensure transparency, governance, and financial security in the global economic system.

Currency Creation and Management

Currency creation and management are at the core of banks' functioning. Banks create currency by providing loans to individuals and businesses while maintaining rigorous balance sheet management. This currency creation is a complex process involving several actors, including central banks, regulators, and governments.

Commercial banks are the main actors in currency creation. They create currency whenever they grant loans by recording a corresponding amount in their clients' accounts. In fact, when a bank grants a loan, it does not need to possess the corresponding funds. Instead, it can create currency by simply recording the corresponding amount in the client's account. This is known as scriptural currency creation.

This currency creation has a significant impact on the economy as it enables financing of investments and projects that stimulate economic growth. However, it can also have negative consequences, particularly during economic or financial crises. Therefore, banks must exercise caution in their currency management, ensuring a balance between risk and profitability.

Central banks play a crucial role in currency management. They regulate the quantity of currency in circulation by setting interest rates and conducting operations in financial markets. They are also responsible for financial stability and consumer protection.

Regulators also play an important role in currency management. They ensure that banks comply with transparency, governance, and security standards by imposing capital requirements and monitoring credit, market, and operational risks.

Finally, governments have a key role in currency management, particularly by setting economic policies aimed at stimulating growth, reducing inflation, and protecting consumers.

Economic Financing

Economic financing is one of the primary missions of banks. Banks offer loans and credit to help businesses, individuals, and governments invest in projects and develop their activities. Banks act as intermediaries between savers and borrowers, collecting deposits and using them to finance profitable projects.

Commercial banks are the main sources of financing for businesses. They provide short-term credit to meet daily cash needs as well as medium and long-term credit for investment projects. Development banks are also important for financing long-term projects, such as public infrastructure and social projects.

Central banks also play a crucial role in economic financing by setting interest rates and implementing monetary policies to regulate economic activity. Central banks can also provide emergency loans to commercial banks during financial crises.

Investment banks provide financing for large corporations and governments by issuing bonds and stocks in financial markets. They also offer advice on mergers and acquisitions and corporate restructuring.

Cooperative banks are financial institutions owned and managed by their members. They offer banking services and loans at favorable interest rates to support small businesses and farmers.

Online banks and neo-banks are new players in the economic financing market. They provide low-cost banking services and facilitate access to financing for individuals and small businesses.

Economic financing is essential for stimulating economic growth and innovation. Banks play a crucial role by providing funds for investment projects. However, banks must manage credit and market risks to ensure financial stability. Financial regulators ensure that banks comply with transparency and governance standards to protect depositors and investors.

The Different Types of Banks

Commercial Banks

Commercial banks are financial institutions that offer basic banking services to individuals and businesses. They are governed by strict regulations to ensure the safety of deposits and the stability of the financial system.

Commercial banks play a crucial role in the economy by mobilizing deposits to finance loans to borrowers, whether individuals or businesses. These banks collect deposits from customers and then use them to grant loans and generate interest.

Banking services offered by commercial banks include current and savings accounts, loans and credits, credit cards, payment services, and electronic currency. Customers can access these services through various distribution channels such as ATMs, physical branches, and online platforms.

Commercial banks are also required to manage the risks associated with their activities. This includes credit risk, which is the risk that borrowers will not repay their debts, as well as market risk, operational risk, liquidity risk, interest rate risk, and foreign exchange risk.

Commercial banks are regulated and supervised by national and international regulatory authorities, which ensure that these institutions comply with transparency and governance standards. Prudential regulatory bodies, such as Basel I, II, and III, have been established to strengthen the financial soundness of banks and minimize systemic risks.

Commercial banks are often criticized for their lack of transparency and limited social responsibility. However, some banks have adopted responsible finance and socially responsible investment (SRI) practices to address the environmental and social concerns of their customers.

Finally, the rise of fintechs and the digitalization of banking services have had a significant impact on commercial banks, which must now adapt to an increasingly competitive environment. Banks have had to innovate and offer new products and services to remain competitive in an ever-changing market.

Investment Banks

Investment banks are financial institutions specializing in market operations, mergers and acquisitions, stock and bond offerings, and financial strategy advisory. Unlike commercial banks, which manage deposits and loans for individuals and businesses, investment banks primarily work with large companies and financial institutions to help them raise funds, manage financial risks, and execute complex transactions.

Investment banks emerged during the 19th century in response to the growing demand for financial expertise for large companies. Over time, their role has evolved, and they have become major players in financial markets, offering services such as trading, portfolio management, and investment advice.

Investment banks are often involved in complex transactions, such as corporate mergers and acquisitions, initial public offerings, bond issuances, and derivatives. They use their expertise to advise companies on how to raise funds, reduce risks, and maximize returns.

However, investment banking activities can also pose risks to the economy due to their involvement in high-risk market operations. This is why they are strictly regulated by financial authorities, particularly in terms of capitalization and risk management.

Ultimately, investment banks play an important role in the functioning of financial markets and the overall economy. Their financial expertise and ability to provide complex financial solutions are valuable assets for large companies and financial institutions. However, their participation in high-risk market activities underscores the importance of regulation and supervision to prevent financial crises.

Central Banks

Central banks play a crucial role in the global economy. Their main mission is the management of monetary policy, which aims to maintain price stability and promote economic growth. Central banks are also responsible for overseeing the banking and financial system of their country and regulating the money market.

Central banks have evolved over time, transitioning from commercial banking institutions to independent government organizations. Most central banks were established in the 19th century to regulate national banking systems, but their role has evolved to include monetary policy and financial stability.

The European Central Bank (ECB) is an example of a central bank created to regulate a common currency. It was established in 1998 to manage the euro and promote financial stability in the Eurozone. The ECB is responsible for defining and implementing the monetary policy of the Eurozone, in collaboration with national central banks.

Central banks use various instruments to influence monetary policy. They can adjust interest rates, buy and sell securities in the money market, and regulate the reserve requirements of commercial banks. Central banks can also intervene in the foreign exchange market to stabilize exchange rates.

Monetary policy has a significant impact on the economy, including inflation, unemployment, and economic growth. Therefore, central banks must work closely with the government and other economic actors to achieve their monetary policy objectives.

Central banks are also responsible for the supervision and regulation of commercial banks and financial institutions. They set solvency and liquidity standards, and ensure that financial institutions comply with regulations on money laundering and terrorist financing.

Finally, central banks have a crucial role to play in preventing and resolving financial crises. They can provide emergency loans to commercial banks and take measures to ensure financial stability in times of crisis.

Development Banks

Development banks are financial institutions specialized in financing economic and social projects aimed at promoting the development of developing countries. Their goal is to support economic growth by financing infrastructure projects, agricultural development programs, energy projects, entrepreneurial initiatives, and other projects that have a positive impact on society.

Development banks can be national or international institutions. National institutions are usually created by governments to support the economic and social development of their country. International institutions, on the other hand, are created by multiple governments or international organizations to finance projects in different countries.

The financing provided by development banks is often cheaper than that of traditional commercial banks, as these institutions have privileged access to low-cost sources of financing such as sovereign funds, institutional investors, and central banks.

Development banks also offer low-interest loans, grants, and guarantees to help businesses access the necessary funding to launch their projects. These institutions can also provide technical assistance to financing recipients to help them develop their projects effectively.

Projects financed by development banks often have positive outcomes for the local economy, as they create jobs, stimulate economic growth, and improve the quality of life for local populations. In addition, development banks can help strengthen the capacities of local public institutions by providing technical assistance to improve public policies and management practices.

Finally, development banks can play a significant role in achieving the United Nations' Sustainable Development Goals by supporting projects that have a positive impact on the environment, health, education, gender equality, and poverty reduction.

Cooperative Banks

Cooperative banks are financial institutions that have the particularity of being owned and managed by their members, often customers who have a close relationship with the bank and share common interests. Unlike other types of banks, which aim to maximize the profits of their shareholders, cooperative banks are non-profit businesses whose mission is to serve the interests of their members and the community.

Cooperative banks were created in the late 19th century to help farmers and agricultural cooperatives access banking services. Today, these banks are present in many countries, mainly in Europe and North America, and are often grouped into cooperative networks that share the same values and principles.

The cooperative model is based on active and democratic member participation in the governance of the bank. Members elect the bank's administrators and have the right to vote on important decisions that concern them. The profits of the bank are redistributed to members in the form of dividends or improved services.

Cooperative banks are often more connected to their community and customers than other types of banks. They often offer products and services tailored to local needs, such as loans for small businesses or microfinance services for low-income individuals. They can also play an important role in financing local and sustainable development projects.

Cooperative banks often have stricter ethical and social standards than other types of banks. They may have policies of not financing controversial sectors such as arms, tobacco, or fossil fuels. They may also engage in sustainable development and poverty reduction projects.

Online Banks and Neo Banks

In an increasingly digital world, online banks and neo banks are gaining popularity among consumers. Online banks are financial institutions that offer banking services exclusively online, without a physical infrastructure, while neo banks are financial startups that offer fully digital banking services.

Online banks and neo banks distinguish themselves from traditional banks by offering fast, convenient, and accessible services at often lower costs. Customers can perform basic banking operations such as bill payment, money transfer, and account management from their computer or mobile phone, without having to physically go to a branch.

However, online banks and neo banks also present risks for consumers, such as data and transaction security, as well as the availability of customer support in case of technical issues. It is therefore important for customers to choose reputable and reliable financial institutions.

In addition, online banks and neo banks may not offer the same advantages as traditional banks, such as loans at favorable rates or personalized financial advisory services. Customers must therefore weigh the cost and benefits of these services before choosing a financial institution.

Finally, online banks and neo banks are in competition with traditional banks, which could lead to changes in the banking sector as a whole. Traditional banks may be compelled to reduce costs and adopt more advanced technologies to remain competitive, which could benefit customers.

Structure and Operation of Banks

Internal Organization

The internal organization of banks is a key element for their efficient operation and success. Banks have a complex structure that includes several departments and functional units. This structure is designed to ensure optimal management of banking operations and to provide quality services to customers.

Most large banks have a similar organizational structure, consisting of three levels: strategic level, tactical level, and operational level. The strategic level is responsible for the overall direction of the bank, the development of policies, and long-term objectives. The tactical level handles the planning and implementation of the bank's strategies, while the operational level is responsible for the execution of day-to-day operations.

Each department in the bank is responsible for specific functions. The banking operations department, for example, handles the management of daily operations such as deposits and withdrawals, fund transfers, and account maintenance. The loans and credits department is responsible for managing loans, assessing risks, and verifying the creditworthiness of borrowers. The finance department is responsible for managing the bank's assets and liabilities, budget planning, and financial risk management.

The internal organization of banks also includes a human

resources department, which handles recruitment, training, and employee development. The compliance department is responsible for ensuring that the bank complies with all regulations regarding legal compliance, anti-money laundering, and international standards.

Internal communication is essential to ensure coordination between different departments and to ensure that the bank's objectives are met. Regular meetings, reports, and evaluat ons are communication tools used to achieve this objective.

Finally, corporate culture is an important element of the internal organization of banks. The bank's values and vision are conveyed to employees through training, communication, and rewarding behaviors that are aligned with the bank's values and vision.

Distribution Channels

Distribution channels are one of the key aspects of bank operations. These channels allow customers to interact with the bank, access its products and services, and carry out financial transactions.

Traditional distribution channels include physical branches, which are usually located in strategic locations to provide easy access to customers. Physical branches allow customers to directly meet with a bank adviser, discuss their financial needs, and conduct transactions. Physical branches also offer additional services such as ATMs, deposit counters, and automatic teller machines.

However, with the evolution of technology, banks have started to use digital distribution channels to reach a wider audience and offer more efficient services. Digital distribution channels include the bank's website, mobile applications, online banking platforms, and chatbots.

Banks' websites provide customers with easy access to information about the bank's products and services, as well as interest rates and credit conditions. Mobile applications allow customers to manage their bank accounts, pay bills, and transfer money from their smartphones or tablets.

Online banking platforms offer a complete banking experience without the intervention of a bank advisor. Customers can open an online account, perform transactions, manage their portfolio, and even invest their money. Chatbots are AI-powered virtual assistants that can help customers with simple questions about their bank accounts or find relevant products and services.

In addition, digital distribution channels offer additional benefits to customers, such as faster response times, lower costs, and additional features like budgeting and financial planning tools.

Therefore, distribution channels are a crucial element of bank operations as they provide an effective means of delivering financial products and services to a wide audience. Banks need to adapt to technological developments to meet the needs of their customers and offer a user-friendly and transparent banking experience.

Risk Management

Risk management is a crucial aspect of banking activities. Banks must manage a multitude of different risks to ensure the safety of their customers, employees, investments, and the entire financial system.

The risks that banks face can be classified into several categories, including credit risk, market risk, operational risk, liquidity risk, interest rate risk, and exchange rate risk. Each type of risk presents specific challenges and requires an appropriate management approach.

Risk management begins with the identification and evaluation of these risks. Banks must determine the probabilities and potential impacts of each type of risk in order to determine the appropriate prevention and control measures.

Banks also employ risk management techniques such as diversification and hedging, securitization, the use of derivatives, modeling, and stress tests to minimize potential risks.

However, risk management cannot be considered a one-time activity. It must be integrated throughout the entire organization and be an ongoing concern for banks. The risk management culture must be ingrained in the values and practices of the company.

Additionally, regulators and supervisory bodies play an important role in risk management by ensuring that banks comply with appropriate regulatory and supervisory standards. Transparency and governance standards are also important to ensure accountability of banks to their customers and society as a whole.

Finally, it should be noted that risk management is a constantly evolving field, with new emerging risks such as cybersecurity and environmental risks. Banks must stay attuned to developments and trends to maintain their ability to effectively manage risks.

Profitability and Financial Performance

Profitability and financial performance are key elements for the long-term survival and growth of banks. In an increasingly competitive economic environment, banks must strive to maximize their profits while effectively managing risks.

Profitability is measured by the return on equity (ROE) and the return on assets (ROA) ratios. ROE measures net profit in relation to equity, while ROA measures net profit in relation to total assets. These ratios help measure the efficiency with which banks use their equity and assets to generate profits.

To increase profitability, banks must seek to maximize their revenues while minimizing their costs. Revenues can be increased through loan growth, fees, and trading income.

Costs can be reduced through better management of operational costs and optimization of risk management.

Financial performance is also measured by other ratios such as liquidity ratio and solvency ratio. The liquidity ratio measures the bank's ability to meet short-term payment obligations, while the solvency ratio measures the bank's ability to withstand potential losses.

To improve their financial performance, banks must seek to increase operational efficiency, effectively manage risks, and maintain an adequate liquidity and solvency ratio. Banks also can look to diversify their product portfolio and develop new products and services to meet changing customer needs.

It is important to note that profitability and financial performance of banks should not be achieved at the expense of ethics and social responsibility. Banks must commit to the highest ethical and environmental standards while seeking to maximize their profitability.

Banking Services and Products

Current and Savings Accounts

Current and savings accounts are basic banking products offered by most banks. Current accounts are used for daily transactions, while savings accounts are used for saving money.

Current accounts allow depositing and withdrawing money, making payments by check or debit card. Current accounts may also offer additional features such as electronic transfers and balance alerts.

Savings accounts are used to save money for future projects or emergencies. These accounts may offer a higher interest rate than current accounts, allowing for earning money on the saved funds. Some savings accounts may also have restrictions on minimum deposits and withdrawals.

Banks also offer more sophisticated savings products, such as fixed-term accounts and savings books. Fixed-term accounts are savings accounts with a fixed interest rate for a specified period. Savings books are savings accounts with a variable interest rate but may offer tax benefits.

It is important to compare offers from different financial institutions to find the savings product that best suits one's needs. Interest rates, fees, and conditions can vary significantly from one bank to another.

It is also important to remember that saving is an important part of financial planning. By saving money regularly, one can build an emergency fund to handle unexpected situations such as job loss or medical expenses. Savings can also be used to achieve long-term financial goals, such as purchasing a house or retirement.

Loans and Credit

Granting loans and credit is one of the primary functions of banks. Loans and credit allow individuals and businesses to acquire goods and services they need, while offering banks opportunities to generate income. In this section, we will explore in detail the different types of loans and credit offered by banks and the implications of their use.

First, it is important to understand the difference between loans and credit. A loan is a sum of money loaned by the bank to a borrower, which must be repaid with interest over a specified period. Credit, on the other hand, is a sum of money made available to the borrower that can be used as needed, with interest charged only on the amount actually used.

Loans and credit are generally classified into two categories: consumer loans and business loans. Consumer loans are intended for individuals to finance personal expenses such as buying a car, real estate, or vacations. Business loans, on the other hand, are intended for businesses to finance their commercial activities, such as purchasing equipment, stocks, or working capital.

There are also mortgage loans used to finance the purchase of real estate property. Mortgage loans can be fixed-rate or variable-rate, depending on the borrower's preference. Student loans are also common and used to finance university studies.

Banks also offer a variety of credit facilities to businesses, such as cash credits to finance daily liquidity needs, leasing arrangements to acquire equipment, and lines of credit for longer-term projects. Banks may also offer consumer credit for unplanned expenses, such as car repairs or medical expenses.

Loans and credit are subject to interest rates that vary depending on the borrower's situation, the type of loan or credit, and the perceived risk by the bank. Interest rates can be fixed or variable, depending on the loan or credit duration and market conditions.

Investment and Wealth Management Services

Investment and wealth management services are key areas of the banking sector. They aim to help clients manage their investments and wealth to achieve their financial goals. Investment services include a range of products such as stocks, bonds, mutual funds, derivative products, etc., which allow clients to diversify their portfolios and achieve optimal returns on their investments. Wealth management, on the other hand, includes services such as tax planning, estate planning, debt management, and cash flow management.

Banks generally offer investment and wealth management services to their affluent clientele, who require personalized guidance in managing their wealth and investments. Banks' investment and wealth management advisors assist clients in understanding the different financial products available, assessing their risk profile, and developing an investment plan that aligns with their long-term financial goals.

It is important to emphasize that investment and wealth management services are not exclusively reserved for affluent clients. Banks also offer online investment services and mutual funds accessible to all types of investors, regardless of their wealth level. These products are often more cost-effective than traditional investment services and are an interesting option for novice investors.

Wealth management can also be a viable option for investors at all levels. Banks often provide financial planning services to help clients develop a wealth management plan tailored to their financial situation. Financial advisors can help clients understand various aspects of financial planning, such as insurance, taxes, and succession, to ensure that their wealth is optimally managed.

Payment Services and Electronic Money

Payment services and electronic money have experienced rapid growth in recent years due to the advancement of technology and changes in consumer habits. Banks play a crucial role in these areas by offering innovative services and products to meet the needs of their clients.

Electronic payment services have evolved to offer a variety of solutions tailored to the needs of businesses and individuals. International money transfers, mobile payments, and electronic wallets are some of the most popular services. International money transfers have significantly reduced transfer costs and times, facilitating trade and fund transfers among family members living in different countries. Mobile payments and electronic wallets also provide increased convenience for online purchases and daily transactions.

Electronic money is another important innovation in the field of payment services. It is often seen as an alternative to traditional currency as it is electronically stored and can be used for online purchases or fund transfers. Electronic money is often associated with prepaid cards or mobile applications that allow users to store electronic funds and use them for making payments.

Banks play a crucial role in the development of electronic money by providing payment and fund transfer solutions. They also provide security services to ensure the confidentiality and security of sensitive financial information. Banks have also expanded their service offerings to include loyalty programs and cashback rewards for transactions made with credit and debit cards.

Furthermore, banks have also partnered with payment technology providers to offer innovative online and mobile payment solutions. For example, some banks have launched mobile payment programs that allow users to pay for purchases using their mobile phones. Other banks have established online payment systems that enable customers to pay bills and transfer funds online.

Insurance and Derivative Products

Insurance and derivative products are financial instruments that have experienced exponential growth in recent decades. Insurance allows for transferring the risk of an unforeseen event (e.g., an accident, fire, or illness) from an individual or a business to an insurance company in exchange for a premium. Derivative products, on the other hand, are financial contracts whose value is derived from an underlying asset (e.g., a stock, a commodity, or a currency).

Insurance is used to cover risks associated with economic, social, and environmental activities. Life insurance, for example, helps protect one's family in case of death or disability. Car insurance, on the other hand, covers the costs of car repairs and replacements in the event of an accident. Home insurance protects against damage to the house and its belongings.

Derivative products, on the other hand, are used to hedge financial and speculative risks. Futures contracts, for example, allow for setting a price for an underlying asset at a future date. Options, on the other hand, grant the right (but not the obligation) to buy or sell an underlying asset at a predetermined price on a specific date.

Derivative products can also be used for speculating on market movements. Hedge funds, for example, often use derivative products to generate high returns by taking long or short positions in financial markets.

Insurance and derivative products have advantages and disadvantages. Insurance allows for risk transfer and protection of stakeholders against financial losses. However, premiums can be costly, especially if the risk is high. Derivative products can help manage financial risks and generate high returns but can also be highly risky and cause significant losses.

Regulation and Banking Supervision

National and International Regulatory Bodies

National and international regulatory bodies play a key role in monitoring and regulating the banking sector. These bodies are responsible for maintaining financial stability, protecting consumers, and preventing systemic risks.

At the international level, the main regulatory bodies are the Bank for International Settlements (BIS), the Basel Committee on Banking Supervision, the International Monetary Fund (IMF), and the Organisation for Economic Co-operation and Development (OECD). These bodies have developed standards and regulations to ensure financial stability, reduce risks, and enhance transparency in the banking sector.

The Basel Committee on Banking Supervision has notably developed three banking regulations agreements, known as Basel I, Basel II, and Basel III. These agreements have established international standards for bank solvency, liquidity, and risk management.

At the national level, each country has its own regulatory body. In France, it is the Prudential Control and Resolution Authority (ACPR) which supervises banks and insurance companies. In the United States, it is the Federal Reserve which is responsible for regulating the banking and financial sector.

National and international regulatory bodies have also established mechanisms for monitoring and resolving banking crises. Deposit guarantee mechanisms allow depositors to recover their money in the event of a bank's failure. Banking crisis resolution mechanisms aim to prevent the spread of systemic risks and maintain financial stability.

Prudential Regulations (Basel I, II, III)

Prudential regulations are standards aimed at limiting the risks incurred by banks and ensuring financial stability. Prudential regulations were developed in response to the 2008 financial crisis, which revealed weaknesses in the banking system. The most significant prudential regulations are the Basel I, II, and III agreements.

Basel I, published in 1988, sets out the capital requirements that banks must hold to cover credit risks. This regulation was put in place to ensure that banks have a solid capital base to withstand unforeseen losses. Basel I was amended in 1996 to include capital requirements for market risks and operational risks.

Basel II, published in 2004, is an improvement on Basel I. It introduces a new method for calculating capital requirements for credit risks, taking into account credit quality, duration, and counterparty risk. Basel II also encourages banks to develop their own credit risk rating systems.

Basel III, published in 2010, is a response to the 2008 financial crisis. It strengthens capital requirements for banks and introduces new liquidity and leverage standards. Basel III also requires banks to consider counterparty risk and liquidity risk in their capital management.

The purpose of prudential regulations is to ensure financial stability and limit the risks incurred by banks. They encourage banks to maintain a solid capital base to cover unforeseen risks, establish strong risk management systems, and comply with liquidity and leverage standards.

However, these regulations are not infallible. They can sometimes be circumvented or poorly enforced. For example, banks may engage in risky practices by using complex financial products or seeking to bypass capital requirements. Therefore, it is important for regulators to remain vigilant and implement effective control and supervision mechanisms to ensure that banks comply with prudential regulations.

Fighting Money Laundering and Terrorism Financing

Fighting money laundering and terrorism financing are major concerns for banks worldwide. These illegal activities can have serious consequences for security, financial stability, and the economy as a whole.

Money laundering involves illegally acquired funds being transformed into clean money through a complex process of financial transactions. Criminals seek to conceal the origin and destination of funds in order to avoid detection by authorities. Terrorism financing, on the other hand, is the use of funds to support terrorist activities, such as purchasing weapons or planning attacks.

Banks are at the forefront of the fight against these illicit activities, as they are often used to conduct financial transactions. Therefore, banks have a responsibility to implement monitoring systems to detect and report suspicious transactions. Authorities can then investigate these transactions and take necessary measures to prevent money laundering and terrorism financing.

To comply with regulations, banks have established anti-money laundering and counter-terrorism financing programs. These programs include policies and procedures to identify customers, assess risks, monitor transactions, and report suspicious activities. Banks must also conduct regular checks to ensure that customers comply with rules and regulations.

National and international regulatory authorities also work with banks to strengthen the fight against money laundering and terrorism financing. Transparency and governance standards have been implemented to help banks detect and report suspicious transactions. Banks must also establish deposit guarantee and crisis resolution systems to protect clients' funds in the event of bankruptcy or crisis.

However, despite all these efforts, the fight against money laundering and terrorism financing remains a challenge for banks. Criminals are constantly seeking new ways to circumvent rules and regulations, making it difficult to detect illicit activities. Therefore, banks must remain vigilant and constantly adapt to ensure the financial security of their clients and the economy as a whole.

Transparency and Governance Standards

Transparency and governance standards are essential to ensure integrity and public trust in the banking sector. In this section, we will explore the different standards and regulations aimed at ensuring transparency and good governance in banks.

First and foremost, transparency is the cornerstone of good governance. Banks must be transparent about their structure, operations, business practices, and risk management. This allows stakeholders, including clients, shareholders, regulators, and the general public, to understand how the bank operates and how it manages its risks.

To ensure this transparency, many regulations have been put in place. For example, the European directive MiFID II (Markets in Financial Instruments Directive) requires banks to disclose detailed information about the financial products they offer, as well as their cost and performance. Similarly, the CRD IV (Capital Requirements Directive IV) directive requires banks to disclose detailed information about their risk profile, capitalization, and risk exposure.

Regarding governance, banks are required to adhere to certain standards to ensure sound and effective management. Firstly, banks must have a clearly defined governance structure, with separate decision-making bodies such as the board of directors and the management committee. The members of these bodies must be independent and competent, with relevant experience in the banking field.

Moreover, banks must establish effective policies to manage risks, including managing conflicts of interest, monitoring regulatory compliance, and managing operational risks such as cybersecurity risks.

Finally, banks must be accountable to their stakeholders, especially their clients and shareholders. To do so, they must establish clear policies regarding information disclosure, complaint management, and fair treatment of clients. They must also be transparent about their financial performance, remuneration policies, and business practices.

Deposit Guarantee and Crisis Resolution Systems

Deposit guarantee and crisis resolution systems are protection mechanisms established by governments and regulatory authorities to ensure the safety of funds deposited by clients in banks. These systems were developed in response to banking and financial crises, which highlighted the need to protect clients from financial losses due to bank failures.

The deposit guarantee system is a mechanism that secures clients' deposits in the event of a bank's failure. It allows clients to recover their funds up to a certain amount, usually set by law. This amount varies from country to country, but is often in the range of several thousand euros. The deposit guarantee system is funded by contributions from banks, calculated based on their risk.

Crisis resolution is a process that addresses the problems of troubled banks while minimizing losses for clients, investors, and taxpayers. Crisis resolution can take various forms, including the sale of the troubled bank to a third party, government recapitalization of the bank, or merger with another bank. Crisis resolution can be costly for taxpayers, which is why it is often accompanied by strict conditions, such as restrictions on executive salaries and measures to protect clients' interests.

Deposit guarantee and crisis resolution systems are essential for maintaining confidence in the banking and financial system. They allow clients to feel secure in depositing their money in a bank, knowing that their funds will be reimbursed in the event of a bank failure. They also help reduce the risk of a banking panic, which can spread rapidly and cause significant losses for clients and investors.

However, it should be noted that these systems have their limits. For example, deposit guarantee systems only cover deposits up to a certain amount, which means that clients depositing higher amounts may incur losses in the event of a bank failure. Moreover, crisis resolution can be challenging to implement in certain cases, especially when banks are too big to fail without causing a systemic crisis.

Typology of banking risks

Credit Risk

Credit risk is one of the major risks that banks are exposed to. It refers to the possibility that a borrower will fail to repay their loan in accordance with the agreed terms, resulting in a loss for the bank. This risk is often present in a bank's loan portfolio and can come from different types of customers, such as businesses, individuals, governments, and non-profit organizations.

Credit risk can be classified into two main categories: default risk and credit quality deterioration risk. Default risk refers to the likelihood that the borrower will not repay the loan, while credit quality deterioration risk refers to the likelihood that the borrower will repay the loan but with a delay or a reduction in the payment amount.

To manage credit risk, banks implement rigorous credit underwriting procedures to ensure that borrowers are able to repay their loan. These procedures include an analysis of the borrower's creditworthiness, an assessment of the collateral provided for the loan, and an evaluation of the economic and sectoral risk associated with the borrower. Banks can also diversify their loan portfolio to reduce their exposure to a specific sector or type of borrower.

In case of default, banks generally have mechanisms in place to recover their money, such as seizing collateral or restructuring the debt. In extreme cases, banks may have to write off losses on their balance sheet.

It is important to note that credit risk is closely related to economic risk. During an economic slowdown, the risk of borrower default increases, which can result in losses for banks.

Market Risk

The concept of market risk is a crucial element in banking activities. Indeed, this type of risk concerns potential losses related to fluctuations in financial markets such as stock markets, currency markets, commodity markets, interest rates, and indices. Banks are therefore exposed to this risk when their portfolio includes financial assets subject to these market variations.

Market risk can be assessed through various methods such as Value-at-Risk (VaR), which quantifies the maximum probable loss of a portfolio at a certain confidence level. Thus, banks use sophisticated mathematical models to estimate their market risk and implement appropriate risk management strategies.

Financial derivatives are often used to hedge market risk. These financial instruments allow the transfer of market risk to a third party. For example, a bank can purchase a futures contract on a commodity to hedge against a price increase. However, the use of these derivative products can also amplify market risk.

Banks must also be aware of the risks associated with complex structured products that can be opaque and difficult to evaluate. Indeed, these products may have hidden risks such as early redemption clauses or buyback options that can result in significant losses for investors.

Finally, banks must also be sensitive to systemic market risks. These risks concern the entire financial system and can be triggered by unpredictable events such as economic and financial crises. Banks must therefore be able to manage these systemic risks by adopting preventive and crisis management measures.

Operational Risk

Operational risk is one of the major risks that banks face. It is defined as the possibility of losses resulting from inappropriate internal processes, human errors, information system failures, fraud, legal disputes, natural disasters, and other unforeseen events. Unlike other types of risks such as credit risk and market risk, operational risk cannot be accurately evaluated or measured, making it difficult to manage.

To better understand the importance of operational risk in banks, it is essential to remember that banks are complex institutions that deal with massive amounts of data and perform a wide range of operations. Failures can occur at any time, and the bank's ability to cope with them depends on its resilience and ability to respond quickly and effectively to events.

In order to manage operational risk, banks have implemented systems and processes for internal control. This includes identifying risks, evaluating internal controls, and implementing risk management measures. Banks must also invest in robust and resilient information systems, as well as in employee training and skill development.

However, despite all the measures taken, operational risks can never be completely eliminated. This is why banks must also have business continuity plans in place to ensure the continuity of services in times of crisis. These plans must be regularly tested and updated to ensure their effectiveness.

Liquidity Risk

Liquidity risk is one of the most important risks that banks face. It refers to the bank's ability to meet its payment obligations when they fall due. In other words, it is the bank's ability to convert its assets into cash quickly and at a low cost to honor customer withdrawals or repay its debts.

Banks face this risk because they collect demand and time deposits and lend money to their customers over longer periods. This maturity mismatch creates a liquidity risk as the bank may not have enough liquid assets to meet its payment obligations.

Banks manage this risk by having careful management of their assets and liabilities and by maintaining sufficient liquidity reserves. Liquidity reserves can take the form of sight deposits with the central bank, tradable securities, or cash.

However, liquidity risk management has become more complex with the evolution of financial markets and the globalization of banking activities. Banks may have difficulty refinancing themselves in the interbank market or in the capital markets in times of financial stress. Moreover, the financial crisis of 2008 emphasized the importance of liquidity management and led to the implementation of stricter regulations to ensure financial stability.

Regulations now require banks to maintain sufficient liquidity buffers to withstand liquidity shocks. In addition, regulators conduct stress tests to assess banks' ability to cope with financial stress scenarios.

Finally, liquidity risk management is essential for customer confidence and financial stability. Banks must be able to meet their customers' liquidity needs at all times to avoid a liquidity crisis. Prudent liquidity management is therefore essential to ensure the soundness of the banking system and prevent financial crises.

Interest Rate Risk

Interest rate risk is a major risk that banks face in their daily activities. This risk is related to fluctuations in interest rates in financial markets, which can have significant impacts on banks' profits and losses.

Specifically, interest rate risk occurs when interest rates increase or decrease significantly and banks' assets and liabilities are not affected in the same way. Banks' assets and liabilities are generally denominated at different interest rates, which creates imbalances when interest rates fluctuate.

For example, if a bank has long-term fixed-rate assets and short-term variable-rate liabilities, an increase in interest rates can lead to increased interest expenses for the bank, while interest income from assets remains fixed. This can result in a decline in profits for the bank.

To manage interest rate risk, banks can use several techniques. They can implement duration matching strategies to align assets and liabilities in terms of duration and interest rate sensitivity. Banks can also use futures contracts and options to hedge against interest rate fluctuations.

However, these risk management techniques are not without risk. Futures contracts and options can be costly, and duration matching strategies can be difficult to implement accurately. Banks must therefore be vigilant in managing their interest rate risk and closely monitor interest rate fluctuations in financial markets.

Finally, it is important to note that interest rate risk not only affects banks but also borrowers and investors. Borrowers can be affected by interest rate fluctuations, which can make loan repayments more expensive or less affordable. Investors can also be affected by interest rate fluctuations, as this can have impacts on the valuation of bond investments.

Foreign Exchange Risk

Foreign exchange risk is an important risk for banks and businesses operating in international markets. It occurs when the value of one currency fluctuates against another, resulting in potential losses for economic actors with open positions in foreign currencies.

To illustrate this risk, let's take the example of a French company selling products in the United States and receiving payments in US dollars. If the euro depreciates against the dollar, the value of the dollar payments received by the company will decrease, as it will need more euros to exchange those dollars into its local currency. This can result in a loss for the company if it has not hedged its foreign exchange risk.

Banks, on the other hand, are often exposed to foreign exchange risk due to their foreign exchange trading activities. If they have open positions in a given currency, an unfavorable fluctuation in the value of that currency can result in significant losses.

To manage foreign exchange risk, both banks and businesses can use hedging instruments such as futures contracts, foreign exchange options, or currency swaps. These instruments allow for the fixing of an exchange rate in advance for a future transaction, thus reducing the risk of currency value fluctuation.

It is important to note that foreign exchange risk can also have consequences for an economy as a whole. For example, a sudden depreciation of the local currency can lead to imported inflation as imported goods become more expensive. This can also make exports more competitive, thus stimulating economic growth.

Risk Management Techniques

Diversification and Hedging

Diversification and hedging are two terms that frequently come up in the banking world, particularly in the context of risk management. Indeed, diversification and hedging are two very important techniques that allow banks to reduce their risks and protect their profitability.

Diversification involves spreading risks across different types of assets, sectors, or geographic regions. In other words, it's about not putting all your eggs in one basket. By diversifying their portfolios, banks reduce the risk of significant losses in the event of the default of a single borrower or a downturn in a single economic sector. For example, a bank that only lends to one sector, such as real estate, can be very vulnerable if real estate prices decline. On the other hand, a bank that lends to multiple sectors, such as agriculture, industry, and services, will be less exposed to sector-specific risk.

Hedging, on the other hand, involves protecting against risks by taking positions opposite to those considered risky. For example, a bank that lends at variable interest rates can hedge against the risk of interest rate increases by entering into financial products that protect against such increases. Similarly, a bank that lends in foreign currencies can hedge against currency exchange risk by purchasing financial products that allow it to protect against a decrease in the value of that currency.

Diversification and hedging are very useful techniques for reducing risks, but they are not foolproof. It is therefore important for banks to implement effective risk management systems to continuously monitor and evaluate the risks taken by the bank.

In summary, diversification and hedging are two essential risk management techniques for banks. By using these techniques, banks can reduce their exposure to specific risks and safeguard their profitability. However, it is important for banks to be aware of the limitations of these techniques and to implement effective risk management systems to continuously monitor and evaluate the risks taken by the bank.

Securitization

Securitization is a financial process that allows banks to transfer a portion of their assets (loans and other financial assets) by bundling them into a portfolio and selling them as securities to investors. The cash flows generated by these securities (repayment of loans, interest, and other income) are then distributed among the investors, who become the owners of the securities.

Securitization offers numerous advantages for banks, including the reduction of their financial risks, the release of capital for new loans, as well as the opportunity to diversify into new markets and financial products. For investors, it provides the opportunity to invest in a diversified portfolio of loans and achieve attractive returns.

However, securitization can also present risks, particularly in case of borrower default, which can lead to a decrease in the value of the securities and losses for the investors. Moreover, the complexity of securitization products can make it challenging to assess their actual risk.

Indeed, the rise of complex securitization products, such as collateralized debt obligations (CDOs), was one of the factors that contributed to the 2008 financial crisis. These products were created by bundling subprime mortgages, which are loans granted to borrowers with high credit risk. Mass defaults on these loans led to a decrease in the value of CDOs and significant losses for the investors holding them.

Thus, it is important for banks and regulators to consider the risks associated with securitization and ensure the implementation of effective regulation and supervision measures to prevent financial abuses. For example, Basel III regulation introduces higher capital requirements for banks engaging in securitization activities in order to reduce their risk of default and increase their financial resilience.

Use of Derivative Products

The use of derivative products is a common practice in the finance and banking industry. These financial instruments are used to manage market, credit, liquidity, and interest rate risks. Derivative products derive their value from an underlying asset, such as stocks, bonds, currencies, commodities, or market indices.

There are several types of derivative products, such as futures contracts, options, swaps, and credit enhancement risk swaps (CERS). Futures contracts allow the purchase or sale of an asset at a pre-determined price on a specific future date. Options provide the right, but not the obligation, to buy or sell an asset at a predetermined price on a fixed future date. Swaps are contracts that exchange financial flows between two parties, while CERS are risk exchange contracts between a bank and a client.

The use of derivative products can be very risky, as their value depends on the performance of the underlying asset. Losses can be substantial if the underlying asset moves unfavorably. Therefore, banks must manage these risks rigorously and prudently by using risk management techniques such as diversification, hedging, securitization, and modeling.

Securitization is a risk management technique that involves transforming illiquid assets into tradable securities in financial markets. This technique allows banks to free up capital by selling the securities to investors. Modeling is a risk management technique that involves simulating possible market scenarios to measure potential losses.

Derivative products can also be used for speculation in financial markets. This can be very profitable, but it can also be very risky. Speculators take positions on derivative products by betting on the future performance of underlying assets. Losses can be substantial if the bet turns out to be incorrect.

Modeling and Stress Tests

Modeling and stress tests are two important tools for risk management in the banking sector. Modeling involves the use of mathematical and statistical methods to predict the bank's future financial outcomes based on different economic scenarios. Stress tests are simulations that assess a bank's resilience to extreme economic shocks.

Modeling helps banks better understand the risks they are exposed to and anticipate market fluctuations. It can also help banks identify investment opportunities and optimize their asset portfolios.

However, modeling also has limitations and risks. It relies on assumptions and models that may be imperfect or inappropriate in certain situations. It can also lead to excessive risk-taking if banks rely too heavily on the results of their models without considering other factors.

This is where stress tests come into play. They test the bank's resilience to extreme economic scenarios, such as a financial crisis or a prolonged recession. Stress tests can also help regulators assess the financial soundness of banks and ensure they have sufficient capital to withstand potential losses.

Stress tests are therefore an important tool to guarantee financial stability and resilience in the banking sector. However, they cannot predict all possible risks and do not alone guarantee a bank's financial security. It is therefore important for banks to adopt a comprehensive and integrated approach to risk management, using a combination of modeling, stress tests, and other risk assessment methods.

The Bank and Monetary Policy

Role of Central Banks

Central banks are important financial institutions that play a crucial role in the global economy. Their main mission is to regulate monetary policy and maintain financial stability.

Central banks have several important functions. First, they are tasked with creating and regulating the quantity of money in circulation in the economy. They are also responsible for managing the country's foreign exchange reserves. This allows them to intervene in foreign exchange markets to maintain exchange rate stability.

Additionally, central banks have an important role to play in maintaining financial stability. They are responsible for monitoring the financial system and taking measures to prevent financial crises. In times of crisis, central banks can also provide emergency liquidity to banks to prevent contagion to the entire financial system.

Central banks also have a mission to maintain price stability. To do this, they use monetary policy instruments such as interest rates and open market operations to regulate the money supply in the economy. High inflation can have adverse consequences on the economy, including reducing the purchasing power of the population and increasing production costs for businesses.

Central banks are also responsible for supervising and

regulat ng commercial banks. They are tasked with ensuring that banks comply with solvency and liquidity standards to ensure their financial stability. They can also take measures to prevent systemic risks such as the risk of contagion between banks.

Finally, central banks play an important role in international relations. They are often involved in negotiations on exchange rates and international economic policies. Central banks also work closely with other central banks to maintain global financial stability.

Monetary Policy Tools

Monetary policy is a major tool that central banks have to achieve their objectives of price stability and economic growth. It involves the use of various instruments to influence the quantity of money in circulation, interest rates, and financing conditions in the economy.

Central banks can use several tools to conduct their monetary policy. The first and most well-known is the key interest rate, which is the rate at which commercial banks can borrow money from the central bank. By changing this rate, central banks can influence the cost of credit and, therefore, economic activity.

Another important tool is open market operations, which involve the buying or selling of government debt securities in the financial market. By buying securities, the central bank injects money into the economy, while selling securities withdraws money from the economy.

Central banks can also use reserve requirements ratios to influence the amount of liquidity that commercial banks must keep in reserve relative to their deposits. By increasing these ratios, central banks can reduce the amount of liquidity available for lending and, therefore, slow down economic activity.

Finally, central banks can also use communication policies to influence the expectations of economic agents. For example, by announcing future interest rate targets or making statements about their future policy, central banks can influence the behavior of economic agents and steer economic activity in the desired direction.

It should be noted that central banks must take into account many factors when deciding on their monetary policy, such as inflation, economic growth, unemployment rate, and market conditions. Therefore, their monetary policy can be complex and difficult to understand for non-specialists.

Impact of Monetary Policy on Banks

The impact of monetary policy on banks is a crucial subject to understand the functioning of the banking system as a whole. Indeed, banks are heavily influenced by the decisions of central banks regarding monetary policy. In this section, we will examine how monetary policy affects banks and how they can respond to it.

Monetary policy is one of the main tools that central banks have to regulate the economy. It involves actions to adjust interest rates and the quantity of money in circulation to maintain economic stability. Central banks can increase or decrease interest rates depending on the state of the economy, which can have a significant impact on banks.

When interest rates increase, borrowing becomes more expensive for banks. This can reduce their ability to lend money, which can lead to a decrease in their revenues and profits. Furthermore, an increase in interest rates can make existing loans more difficult for borrowers to repay, which can lead to an increase in defaults. As a result, banks may face higher loan-related losses, which can affect their financial health.

Conversely, when interest rates decrease, it can stimulate borrowing and economic growth. It can also increase banks' profits as they can lend money at lower rates and earn higher returns on bond investments. However, a decrease in interest rates can also increase risks for banks as they may be tempted to lend to high-risk borrowers to generate higher returns.

Banks can respond to the impact of monetary policy in several ways. They can adjust their lending rates to reflect changes in central bank interest rates. They can also modify their loan portfolios to reduce the risks associated with interest rate fluctuations. Additionally, they can turn to other sources of funding, such as capital markets, to obtain funds at competitive interest rates.

Lastly, banks can use derivatives products to hedge against interest rate fluctuations. Derivatives are financial instruments that allow banks to transfer risks related to interest rate fluctuations to other parties. This can help reduce banks' exposure to interest rate risks and maintain their profitability.

Relationship between Monetary Policy and Financial Stability

Monetary policy and financial stability are closely related. Monetary policy refers to the measures taken by central banks to influence the quantity of money in circulation and interest rates in the economy. The main objective of monetary policy is to maintain price stability, i.e., a low and stable level of inflation. However, the actions of the central bank can also have significant impacts on financial stability.

Financial stability refers to the ability of the financial system to withstand economic shocks and prevent financial crises. Financial stability is essential to ensure the proper functioning of the economy and to avoid the disastrous consequences of financial crises, such as bank failures, economic recessions, and mass unemployment.

Monetary policy can impact financial stability in different ways. First, monetary policy decisions can influence the volatility of prices of financial assets such as stocks, bonds, and currencies. Changes in interest rates can also affect the solvency of businesses and households, which can have implications for financial stability.

Moreover, monetary policy can also impact the behavior of financial market participants, such as investors, banks, and financial institutions. For example, low interest rates can encourage investors to take excessive risks by investing in riskier assets to obtain higher returns. This can lead to increased volatility in the financial market and increase the risk of a financial crisis.

In addition, monetary policy can also have implications for the regulation and supervision of the financial system. Regulators must closely monitor the impact of monetary policy measures on financial stability and take measures to mitigate risks.

Finally, coordination between monetary policy and macroprudential policy is essential to maintain financial stability. Macroprudential policy comprises measures taken to mitigate systemic risks in the financial system. This includes the regulation and supervision of banks, the management of liquidity risks, and monitoring the evolution of asset prices. Coordination between monetary policy and macroprudential policy is crucial to ensure financial stability.

Banks and Financial Markets

Introduction to Financial Markets and Their Role

Financial markets are places where financial securities such as stocks, bonds, derivatives, and currencies are traded. These markets play a crucial role in the economy, as they allow companies, governments, and individuals to finance their projects by obtaining capital from investors. They also offer investors a way to diversify their portfolio and realize gains by investing in securities that have potential for growth.

Financial markets have evolved over time to become complex systems that are interconnected with the global economy. They are composed of different financial institutions such as stock exchanges, brokers, investment banks, and pension funds. These institutions facilitate financial transactions between market participants.

The primary role of financial markets is to facilitate the flow of money and financial securities. They allow companies to raise funds by issuing stocks or bonds, which are then purchased by investors. Governments can also raise funds by issuing government bonds.

Financial markets are also a means of transferring risks. Investors can purchase derivatives to hedge against market risks such as fluctuations in interest rates or commodity prices. Investment banks can also buy derivatives to transfer risks from their portfolios to other investors.

Financial markets also play an important role in determining the prices of financial assets. Prices are determined by supply and demand, and are influenced by various factors such as economic data, political events, global events, and company announcements. Investors can use technical analysis and fundamental analysis to evaluate assets and make investment decisions.

Financial Instruments and Derivatives

Financial instruments and derivatives are complex financial tools that have revolutionized the world of finance in recent decades. Derivatives are financial contracts whose value depends on an underlying asset such as stocks, currencies, commodities, or interest rates. Financial instruments are negotiable debt securities such as stocks, bonds, investment certificates, warrants, and options. Banks are major players in the markets for these financial instruments and derivatives.

Derivatives offer many advantages to investors, such as the ability to hedge against price fluctuations, speculate or changes in the value of underlying assets, diversify their portfolio, and maximize their returns. However, these financial instruments are also very risky, as they can cause significant losses and even financial crises.

The 2008 financial crisis highlighted the risks associated with the excessive use of derivatives, particularly Credit Default Swaps (CDS), which contributed to the bankruptcy of some major banks. Since then, regulators have taken measures to limit the risks associated with these financial instruments, including strengthening capital requirements and imposing limits on banks' positions.

Financial instruments, on the other hand, have been widely used by companies to raise funds and finance themselves at a lower cost. Stocks are financial instruments that represent ownership in a company and offer rights such as voting rights and dividend rights. Bonds, on the other hand, are debt securities that represent a debt to be repaid to the investor. Banks can issue these financial instruments to finance their activities or sell them to their clients.

Banks also play an important role in capital markets, where they act as brokers, market makers, and underwriters of stock and bond issuances. Banks can also invest in investment funds and private equity firms to generate returns for their clients.

Finally, the use of digital technologies and innovations such as blockchain and smart contracts is likely to radically transform the markets for financial instruments and derivatives. Banks must therefore closely monitor these technological developments to remain competitive and offer innovative services to their clients.

Interaction between Banks and Financial Markets

The interaction between banks and financial markets is close and complex. Banks have close ties to financial markets as they play key roles as financial intermediaries, issuers of debt and equity, lenders, and investors. Financial markets, on the other hand, provide liquidity and sources of funding for banks.

Banks interact with financial markets in several ways. Firstly, banks can be active in financial markets by buying and selling financial assets such as stocks, bonds, currencies, and derivatives. Secondly, banks issue debt on financial markets by selling bonds, negotiable debt securities, and other debt instruments. Thirdly, banks can lend money to businesses or individuals using funds raised from financial markets.

Financial markets can also affect banks in several ways. Price movements in financial markets can have significant effects on banks' securities portfolios and financial results. For example, interest rate movements can affect the value of banks' assets and liabilities, and therefore their net income. Exchange rate movements can also have a significant impact on the financial results of banks operating in international markets.

Banks and financial markets may be interdependent, but this does not mean that they are always in harmony. Financial crises can arise when banks and financial markets are faced with external shocks that simultaneously affect them. For example, the global financial crisis of 2008 was triggered by the bankruptcy of major investment banks and led to a liquidity crisis in financial markets.

Investment Banks and Their Activities

Investment banks are financial institutions that provide investment advisory services and underwriting services for securities issuances to companies, governments, and financial institutions. These services are intended to help clients raise capital in financial markets, manage financial risks, and acquire or sell financial assets.

Investment banks differ from commercial banks in their focus on market activities rather than loans and deposits. They often work with clients with more sophisticated financial needs, such as large companies, hedge funds, and institutional investors.

The activities of investment banks include investment advisory, asset management, securities trading, underwriting of securities issuances, and creation of structured financial products. Investment advisory involves providing recommendations to clients on how to manage their portfolio and make investment decisions. Asset management involves managing investment portfolios for clients, such as pension funds or institutional investors.

Securities trading involves buying and selling securities in financial markets to generate profits for the investment bank. Underwriting of securities issuances involves helping clients issue new securities in financial markets by finding buyers for these securities. The creation of structured financial products involves designing and selling complex financial products, such as credit derivatives, which can be used to hedge financial risks.

Investment banks have also been involved in controversial activities such as securitization of mortgage loans, which contributed to the 2008 financial crisis. Since this crisis, regulators have imposed stricter restrictions on the activities of investment banks.

Technological Innovations and Their Impact on the Banking Sector

The Rise of Fintechs

In recent years, fintechs have played a significant role in the financial industry. Fintechs are technology startups that use technology to offer innovative financial services to consumers. These companies have disrupted the traditional financial market by providing services that are faster, more efficient, and more accessible than traditional banks.

Fintechs have developed user-friendly mobile applications that allow users to manage their money in real time, make instant bank transfers, invest in the stock market, and securely manage their portfolio. Fintechs have also developed cutting-edge technologies such as artificial intelligence and blockchain to offer faster and more accessible loan, insurance, and payment services.

These innovations have not only changed the way financial services are offered but have also created competition for traditional banks. Fintechs have attracted customers thanks to their more innovative and personalized services, as well as their often lower fees compared to traditional banks. Consumers can now access financial services without the need to visit a physical bank branch.

However, fintechs are not without risks. Consumers must be aware of the risks associated with using these services, such as data security, fraud, and the risk of financial loss. Financial regulators have also taken measures to oversee fintech activities in order to protect consumers and ensure financial stability.

Despite the risks, fintechs continue to gain popularity and have become a driver of innovation in the financial industry. Traditional banks are now forced to innovate in order to remain competitive and meet the needs of their customers. Fintechs have also created new business models, leading to partnerships between traditional banks and fintechs to offer more innovative and efficient financial services.

The Digitalization of Banking Services

The digitalization of banking services is one of the key changes currently taking place in the banking industry. Technological advances have led to the emergence of new payment solutions, new financial service offerings, new communication channels, and new means of wealth management. This digitalization has extended to all banking activities, from account opening to risk management.

The digitalization of banking services has made access to financial services easier, faster, and safer for customers. Traditional banks have started offering mobile applications to facilitate account management, online payments, and transaction history viewing. These applications have simplified the subscription process and offered service offerings that are more tailored to customer needs.

Fintechs have also emerged as an alternative to traditional banks, offering exclusively online banking services. These neobanks have managed to attract many customers thanks to competitive offers and innovative services. Neobanks offer personalized services, more attractive credit offerings, and highly advanced budget management features.

The digitalization of banking services has also led to the emergence of new payment solutions, such as mobile payment and electronic currency. These new solutions have simplified payment processes, reduced transaction costs, and increased transaction security. Mobile payment solutions have become popular among consumers who appreciate their simplicity and convenience.

The digitalization of banking services has also improved risk management. Banks now use sophisticated tools to assess credit and market risks, as well as to monitor suspicious activities. Banks have also invested in cybersecurity to protect their customers' personal data and prevent fraud.

Finally, the digitalization of banking services has expanded access to financial services, particularly in developing countries. Fintechs have launched microfinance initiatives to support small businesses and populations excluded from the traditional banking system. Online banks and neobanks have also reduced transaction costs and offered accessible financial services for all.

Cryptocurrencies and Blockchain

Cryptocurrencies and blockchain are increasingly prevalent topics in the world of finance and banking. Cryptocurrencies are digital currencies that are usually decentralized and not regulated by a central bank or government entity. Blockchain, on the other hand, is an information storage and transmission technology that functions as a public and decentralized ledger.

While these technologies are still relatively new, they have the potential to revolutionize the banking sector by offering an alternative to traditional methods of money management. Cryptocurrencies can provide increased security and transparency, as well as cost reduction for money transfers and cross-border transactions. Blockchain can also offer increased transaction security and transparency by reducing the risks of fraud and hacking.

However, cryptocurrencies and blockchain are also associated with significant risks. Cryptocurrencies are still relatively volatile, with significant and unpredictable price fluctuations. The decentralized nature of cryptocurrencies also means that recovering lost or stolen funds can be difficult. Blockchain is also vulnerable to cyber attacks, although it is considered more secure than traditional data storage methods.

Banks are starting to integrate cryptocurrencies and blockchain into their service offerings. Some banks have begun to offer accounts for cryptocurrency investors, as well as blockchain-based payment options. Some banks also use blockchain technology for internal operations management.

Artificial Intelligence and Robotization

Artificial intelligence (AI) and robotization have become prominent topics in the banking sector in recent years. Technological advancements have allowed banks to become more efficient and profitable by automating certain repetitive tasks.

AI is a technology that enables machines to learn and improve based on the data they process. In the banking sector, AI is used to automate tasks such as customer background verification, credit risk assessment, and fraud detection. It can also be used to assist customers in making financial decisions by providing personalized advice based on their profile and goals.

Robotization, on the other hand, allows for the automation of more physical tasks such as cash management and document handling. It also improves the speed and efficiency of banking processes.

These technological advancements have consequences for bank employees. Some tasks that were once performed by humans can now be done by machines, which can lead to job losses. However, automation also allows employees to focus on more complex and value-added tasks.

AI and robotization also have implications for bank customers. On one hand, they can enable banks to better understand their customers' needs and offer more tailored products and services. On the other hand, they can also lead to cost reductions, which can translate into lower banking fees for customers.

However, the use of AI and robotization also raises ethical and security concerns. Customer data must be protected, and the algorithms used to make decisions must be transparent and fair.

The Challenges of Cybersecurity

Cybersecurity is a major concern for modern banks, which must protect their customers' data, financial transactions, and their own computer systems. Banks are prime targets for hackers and cybercriminals, who seek to exploit security vulnerabilities to gain access to confidential information, steal money, or disrupt banking activities.

To address these threats, banks must implement effective security measures, using state-of-the-art technologies to detect and prevent attacks, as well as training their staff in managing IT risks. Cybersecurity is a constant concern for banks, which must remain vigilant in the face of evolving threats and technologies.

Banks must also comply with cybersecurity standards and regulations, following the guidelines of national and international regulatory bodies. They must have business continuity plans in place to ensure the availability of banking services in the event of a security incident, and they must be transparent with their customers about the security measures they have in place to protect their data.

The cybersecurity challenges for banks are manifold, ranging from protecting customer privacy to preserving financial stability. Banks must be able to detect and prevent cyber attacks while ensuring the availability of banking services and protecting customer data. To do so, they must invest in cutting-edge technologies and train their staff in managing IT risks.

In conclusion, cybersecurity is a crucial issue for modern banks, which face a constant and ever-evolving threat. Banks must be able to protect their computer systems, financial transactions, and customer data while complying with security standards and regulations.

The Bank and the International Economy

Banks in International Trade

Banks play a crucial role in international trade by providing essential financial services to businesses and governments. Banks are often involved in financing international trade by offering products such as letters of credit, guarantees, and documentary credits. Banks are also frequently involved in settling international payments, facilitating fund transfers between parties involved in international trade transactions.

Banks can also help businesses manage exchange rate risk by offering financial products such as forward contracts and options. These products allow companies to protect themselves against fluctuations in exchange rates and manage their exposure to exchange rate risks.

Banks also have an important role to play in financing infrastructure and projects overseas. Development banks, for example, can provide funding for infrastructure and development projects in developing countries. Commercial banks can also be involved in financing projects abroad by offering long-term loans and structured financing.

Banks are also involved in financing international trade of commodities such as oil and metals. Banks can assist businesses in financing the purchase of commodities by providing structured financing and acting as brokers for commodity futures contracts.

However, banks are also exposed to risks in international trade, such as credit risk and exchange rate risk. Therefore, banks must be able to manage these risks effectively and prudently.

The Role of Banks in Financial Crises

The role of banks in financial crises is a crucial subject for understanding how banks can influence and contribute to economic instability. Financial crises have been significant events in recent economic history, and banks have often been blamed as one of the major causes of these crises.

During financial crises, banks tend to be involved in several ways. One of the main causes is excessive lending. Banks have often granted loans to borrowers who cannot repay them, creating credit bubbles and excessive debt. Banks have also been involved in speculative activities in financial markets, often using complex financial products such as derivatives. Banks have also engaged in inappropriate and opaque risk management practices, creating significant systemic risks for the economy.

When these credit bubbles burst and risks materialize, banks can find themselves in trouble. If borrowers cannot repay their debts, banks can incur significant losses, which can lead to bank failures and financial crises. These crises can also spread throughout the entire financial system, creating a broader economic crisis.

In this context, central banks and financial regulators have a crucial role to play in mitigating the risks and effects of financial crises. Central banks can act as lenders of last resort for troubled banks, providing liquidity to prevent bank failures. Financial regulators can also play an important role by limit ng risky practices of banks and requiring sufficient reserves to address risks.

However, it is important to emphasize that banks are not the sole responsible parties for financial crises. Other actors, such as governments, financial regulators, and investors, also have a role to play in preventing and mitigating the effects of financial crises.

Monetary Policy and Central Banks

Monetary policy is a set of measures implemented by central banks to influence the quantity of money in circulation and regulate the economy. Central banks have a crucial role in a country's financial and economic stability.

One of the main functions of central banks is to control the supply of money in circulation. To do this, they use several tools, such as setting interest rates, buying and selling government securities in the markets, or regulating the required reserves of commercial banks. The objective is to influence the behavior of economic agents (households, businesses, banks) to promote economic growth while limiting inflation.

The impact of monetary policy on banks is considerable.

Commercial banks are the primary beneficiaries of the measures implemented by central banks. For example, when the central bank lowers interest rates, it makes credit cheaper, stimulating credit demand and potentially leading to increased bank deposits. This can enable banks to generate higher profits.

However, banks can also be negatively affected by monetary policy measures. For instance, an increase in interest rates can make loans more expensive, discouraging borrowers and reducing bank deposits. This can result in a decrease in bank profits and affect their ability to grant loans.

Central banks also play an important role in financial stability. They are responsible for supervising and regulating commercial banks, as well as managing bank crises. Central banks implement deposit guarantee policies and crisis resolution measures to prevent bank panics and preserve depositor confidence.

Monetary policy and central banks also have a key role in international exchanges. Fluctuations in exchange rates can have significant effects on the economy and trade of a country. Central banks can intervene in foreign exchange markets to stabilize exchange rates and prevent abrupt variations.

The Ethical and Environmental Challenges

Responsible Finance and Socially Responsible Investment (SRI)

Responsible finance and socially responsible investment (SRI) are relatively recent concepts in the banking world, but they are becoming increasingly important for consumers and investors concerned about the social and environmental impact of their financial choices.

Socially responsible investment (SRI) is an investment approach that aims to invest in companies that adhere to social, environmental, and governance (ESG) criteria. This approach takes into account the impacts of companies on society and the environment in the selection of investments.

Banks have a key role to play in socially responsible investment by offering financial products and services that incorporate ESG criteria. Banks can also raise awareness among their clients by informing them about the benefits cf socially responsible investment.

Responsible finance is a broader approach that takes into account the impacts of financial institutions on society and the environment. Banks can integrate ESG criteria into their own operations and investment strategies to have a positive impact on society and the environment.

For example, banks can finance projects that have a positive impact on the environment, such as renewable energy or biodiversity conservation. They can also commit to reducing their own carbon footprint by using renewable energy in their operations and reducing energy consumption.

Responsible finance and socially responsible investment are not only ethical approaches, but they can also be profitable. Companies that meet ESG criteria can be more resilient and perform better in the long term, as they are better equipped to deal with environmental and social risks.

Banks and the Fight against Climate Change

Banks play an important role in the fight against climate change. By financing environmentally friendly projects, they can help reduce greenhouse gas emissions and promote the transition to a greener economy.

However, banks have long been criticized for their lack of commitment to the environment. Today, more and more banks are realizing the urgency of the situation and are committing to finance sustainable and responsible projects.

These initiatives can take various forms, such as implementing loan policies that favor green projects, investing in sustainable funds, or creating specific financial products to finance the energy transition.

However, it is important to note that the fight against climate change should not be seen as a mere business opportunity for banks. It is a crucial issue for the planet and future generations.

Therefore, it is essential for banks to commit to strict environmental standards and adopt sustainable practices in their daily activities. This can include initiatives such as reducing greenhouse gas emissions from their own operations, implementing recycling policies, or using renewable energy.

Finally, it is important to emphasize that the fight against climate change can only be achieved collectively. Banks have a role to play, but it is also crucial for governments, businesses, and citizens to commit to reducing their carbon footprint and supporting the transition to a greener economy.

Microfinance and Financial Inclusion

Microfinance is an essential tool for promoting financial inclusion in developing countries. It involves providing financial services to people who do not have access to traditional banking services, such as loans, savings, and money transfers. The beneficiaries of microfinance are often micro-entrepreneurs, small farmers, and self-employed workers who seek to develop their economic activity or invest in their own education or that of their children.

Microfinance is often associated with microfinance institutions (MFIs), which are organizations that provide these financial services. MFIs were created to fight poverty and help the poorest individuals become economically self-sufficient.

These institutions emerged in the 1970s in Latin America and Asia and have experienced rapid growth in recent decades.

MFIs have a significant impact on the lives of vulnerable populations in developing countries. The loans they provide allow entrepreneurs to start or expand their businesses, purchase equipment, or stock products. The savings offered by MFIs allow individuals to set aside money for difficult times and invest in their future. Money transfers enable migrant workers to support their families back home.

Microfinance also has a positive impact on society as a whole. It contributes to reducing poverty, creating jobs, and stimulating the local economy. It also builds trust among populations in financial institutions and facilitates access to other financial services such as insurance and credit for larger businesses.

However, microfinance is not without risks. MFIs face challenges such as loan repayment, risk management, funding their own growth, and regulation. They must also demonstrate transparency and accountability to ensure the trust of investors and beneficiaries.

Despite these challenges, microfinance continues to grow and have a positive impact on vulnerable populations in developing countries. It has become an essential tool for promoting financial inclusion and enabling those in need to realize their economic potential.

Future Perspectives for the Banking Sector

Challenges and Opportunities for Traditional Banks

Traditional banks are facing numerous challenges and opportunities in an ever-changing economic and technological environment. The challenges for traditional banks include increasing competition from neobanks and fintech companies, evolving regulations, margin pressures, and the need to continue innovating to meet customer needs.

Growing competition from neobanks and fintech companies is one of the major challenges for traditional banks. Neobanks and fintech companies have lower operating costs and are often more agile in meeting customer needs. They also offer innovative products and services that attract customers looking for a more personalized and digital banking experience.

Another challenge for traditional banks is the evolution of regulations. Regulations are becoming increasingly strict, making it difficult for traditional banks to maintain profitability while adhering to compliance standards. Banks need to be able to navigate new regulations while ensuring that compliance does not hinder their ability to innovate and provide competitive products and services.

Margin pressures are also a challenge for traditional

banks. Traditional banks are facing margin pressures due to declining interest rates, increased competition, and high compliance costs. Banks need to be able to manage their costs while maintaining healthy margins.

However, traditional banks also have opportunities to seize. One such opportunity is the ability to offer complementary products and services to customers. Traditional banks have an established relationship with their customers and can leverage this relationship to offer services such as wealth management, mortgages, and insurance. This allows banks to diversify their sources of income and maintain healthy margins.

Traditional banks also have the opportunity to adapt to technological advancements. Banks can utilize artificial intelligence, blockchain, and other technologies to enhance operational efficiency, provide more personalized services, and improve the customer experience. Traditional banks can also leverage customer data to enhance their services and products.

The Future of Banks in the Face of Technological Advancements

The future of banks is closely tied to the rapid evolution of technology. Financial technology (fintech) companies and technology giants such as Google, Apple, Facebook, Amazon (GAFA) are disrupting the traditional banking sector. Banks are facing increasing competition and must quickly adapt to technological advancements to remain competitive. In this section, we will explore the main trends and challenges that banks will face in the coming years.

Firstly, digitization is radically transforming how banks interact with their customers. Online and mobile banking services are becoming increasingly popular, allowing customers to manage their accounts and conduct transactions from anywhere and at any time. Banks must invest in robust and user-friendly digital platforms to meet their customers' needs.

Furthermore, banks must prepare for the arrival of disruptive technologies such as blockchain and cryptocurrencies. Blockchain, a distributed ledger technology enabling decentralized and transparent transactions, has the potential to significantly reduce transaction costs and processing times. Banks must explore the opportunities offered by blockchain and cryptocurrencies while managing the risks associated with these emerging technologies.

Banks must also invest in artificial intelligence (AI) and machine learning to enhance their data processing capabilities. AI algorithms can help banks detect fraud, assess credit risks, and personalize product and service offerings for their customers. However, banks must also be aware of the risks associated with the use of AI, such as algorithmic discrimination and bias.

Lastly, banks must focus on cybersecurity to protect their customers' data and prevent data breaches. Cyberattacks are becoming increasingly sophisticated, and banks must invest in cutting-edge technologies to safeguard their systems and data.

Emerging Trends and Business Models

Emerging trends and business models in the banking sector are constantly evolving and impacting how banks interact with their customers and manage their operations. Technological advancements are at the core of these changes, enabling banks to offer more efficient and personalized services. Here are some key trends to consider:

- Online banking: Online banks have revolutionized the banking sector by offering a convenient alternative to traditional banks. By providing fully online services, these banks have eliminated geographical constraints and allowed customers to manage their accounts and conduct transactions from anywhere in the world.

- Artificial intelligence and automation: Banks are increasingly using artificial intelligence to automate data processing and analyze customer data to provide more personalized products and services. Chatbots and other virtual assistants are also being used to respond to customer inquiries in real-time.

- Blockchain: Blockchain technology allows banks to securely transfer funds without the need for trusted intermediaries such as central banks. This enables banks to reduce transaction costs and accelerate processing times.

- Mobile payments: Mobile payments are becoming the norm in many countries. Banks are offering mobile applications that allow customers to conduct secure transactions using their smartphones.

- Neobanks: Neobanks are startups offering innovative banking services, such as free current accounts and personalized credit cards. These new companies are disrupting the traditional banking sector by offering more flexible and cost-effective solutions.

- Bank-fintech partnerships: Banks are increasingly partnering with fintech companies to offer innovative services to their customers. Fintech companies bring technological expertise that banks can leverage to enhance their services, while banks provide customer bases and financial expertise.

- Automated investment offerings: Banks are increasingly offering automated investment offerings, called «robo-advisors.» These services use algorithms to analyze customer data and provide personalized investment recommendations.

Acknowledgment

Dear readers,

Firstly, I would like to thank you for taking the time to read this book. I hope that this book has allowed you to discover and better understand the fascinating world of banking.

I would also like to express my gratitude to all banking and finance professionals who have contributed to the writing of this book by sharing their experiences and expertise. Your knowledge and passion for the subject have been a source of inspiration and enrichment for this book.

I strongly believe that understanding banking and financial mechanisms is essential to comprehend the functioning of the global economy and make informed decisions in our daily lives.

Finally, I would like to express my appreciation to all the sources that have been consulted and referenced in the writing of this book. These sources have helped support the presented arguments and ensure the quality and reliability of the information provided.

In conclusion, I hope that you have enjoyed reading this book as much as I have enjoyed writing it. I wish you continued success and encourage you to continue learning about the banking and financial world, a field that is constantly evolving.

Sincerely,